CW01084194

The start of the Second World War was marked by the sinking of the British liner *Athenia* on 3 September 1939 by a U-boat. The war ended with the surrender of the German U-boat fleet in Londonderry on 14 May 1945. In the intervening six years the Battle of the Atlantic – the longest battle of the war – was waged on the cruel seas between Europe and America.

This publication is part of a series which looks at the contribution which the people of Northern Ireland played in the Second World War in service abroad as well as on the home front. Fermanagh played a vitally important role.

Joe O'Loughlin was brought up in Belleek in the Donegal Corridor and well remembers the roar of the flying-boats as they made their way to and from the Atlantic. John Hughes lived in Irvinestown and Enniskillen after the war. Both use their respective experiences and memories in recording the wartime role of Fermanagh.

In writing this monograph the authors have drawn extensively from publications by Breege McCusker, Ian Henderson, Guy Warner and Ernie Cromie, whose researches are acknowledged with thanks. Brian Barton, Ernie Cromie and Richard Doherty provided constructive comment and corrected inaccuracies. John McMillan applied his design skills in laying out the text.

Lieutenant Colonel C T Hogg
Northern Ireland War Memorial

Cover image: Imperial War Museum CH 15350

1   BATTLE OF THE ATLANTIC

Prelude to the Second World War

The attack on Pearl Harbor on 7 December 1941 by the Japanese Navy was intended as a reprisal against a US-led trade embargo on Japan. The strike against the US naval base in Hawaii resulted in the destruction of 188 aircraft, while eight battleships and eleven other vessels were sunk or damaged. Fortunately the aircraft carriers were not in the harbour. However, the US Navy was caught off guard on a day which President Franklin D Roosevelt described as 'a date which will live in infamy'.

The attack on the Pacific Fleet came as a profound shock to the American people. On 11 December 1941 Germany and Italy declared war on the USA, which was reciprocated by the USA on the same day. This led directly to the American entry into both the Pacific and European theatres. Domestic support for non-intervention waned but did not disappear, as there were American politicians who continued to oppose the USA's involvement in the war.

An agreement in March 1941 to allow US bases in the UK was related to the US Navy's protection of convoys and the American intention to help in escorting convoys the full way across the Atlantic. Hitherto, US Navy escorts had been provided only as far as Iceland, or to the mid-ocean meeting point (MOMP).

The USA agreed to build four bases in Britain, two for escort ships and two for flying-boats, with one each in Northern Ireland and Scotland. These were: Base I at Londonderry and Base II at

Rosneath near Glasgow (both for escort ships), Base A at Lough Erne and Base B at Loch Ryan (both for flying-boats). There were two escort ship bases and two flying-boat bases to provide alternative facilities in the event of German bombing forcing the closure of any of the bases.

About 400 'technicians' (some were parolees from federal and state prisons) arrived in Londonderry on 30 June 1941. Others followed but the major work on the Londonderry base was not completed until September 1942. Technicians also arrived at Lough Erne around the same time to commence construction of a flying-boat base for the US Navy. Manual labour was recruited locally and all labour costs were met by the British government.

At a meeting in Washington in December 1941 between President Roosevelt and Prime Minister Churchill, it was agreed that all defensive activity in Northern Ireland, with the exception of the balloon barrages at Londonderry and Belfast, should be taken over by American forces, with USAAF pursuit, or fighter squadrons relieving RAF Fighter Command. These plans were abandoned in 1942 as a result of the decision to attack the Axis powers in North Africa, as were the plans for US troops to take over the defence of Northern Ireland.

The US Navy's main base was in Londonderry. Following the bombing of Pearl Harbor, the US Navy abandoned its plans for four sites. In Fermanagh the flying boat base at Castle Archdale and the repair facility at Killadeas came under RAF control, while the ammunition depot at Kiltierney (near Kesh) and the hospital at Necarne Castle (Irvinestown), were handed over to the US Army.

Fermanagh Bases

The bases for the flying-boats in Lough Erne were Castle Archdale and Killadeas, which opened in February 1941. No. 240 Squadron with obsolete Supermarine Stranraer biplane flying-boats was the first unit to be based there. Land planes operated from St Angelo. Lough Erne had been surveyed from the air on Christmas Day 1940 to see if it was suitable as a base for flying-boats, being the most westerly part of the UK. A water location was necessary as

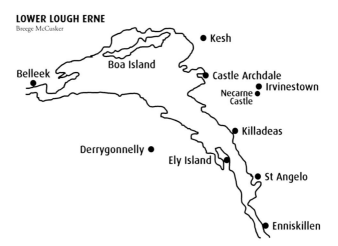

the main aircraft in use at the time for protecting the convoys in the Atlantic were long range flying-boats.

Lough Erne met this requirement. It would have taken at least a year to construct a land base, but in Lough Erne there was a ready-made runway. It was one of only a few inland water bases which could be used in most kinds of weather, as coastal waters were often subject to adverse weather conditions.

The Black Pit

Due to the proximity of German U-boat bases in France from June 1940 and air attacks from Fw 200 Condors, it was considered too dangerous for shipping to use St George's Channel and the Irish Sea to get into Merseyside, the Clyde and other ports without protection. Convoys using the north Atlantic route had the protection of Allied warships based in Londonderry and Belfast Lough, as well as long-range land planes based in Counties Londonderry and Antrim.

From the outset of war, German U-boats roamed the Atlantic at almost free rein, sinking several hundred ships with the loss of massive quantities of supplies and the deaths of untold numbers of seamen and passengers.

A large area in mid-Atlantic – known as the 'Black Pit' by the Royal Navy and RAF – could not be reached by planes from the UK, Iceland or Canada until very long range B-24 Liberators began to operate from Northern Ireland and Iceland.

Furthermore, the U-boats were able to extend their range as far as the east coast of America by the use of large tanker U-boats from which smaller vessels could refuel. There was one case of a U-boat going up the St Lawrence River and torpedoing convoy ships assembled there.

Lough Erne had, however, one major problem. It did not provide direct access to the Atlantic. A 200-mile return journey to Londonderry had to be added to gain access to the Atlantic Ocean. This reduced the time available for patrolling and the effective range of the aircraft. The solution was to seek permission from the Eire government to gain direct access to the Atlantic through County Donegal.

An agreement was reached between the Eire Government and Sir John Maffey, the British representative in Dublin, in January 1941, permitting Lough Erne based flying-boats to cross over the four-mile section of Irish neutral territory from Belleek to Ballyshannon, and the three-mile territorial waters of the state. They had to keep

DONEGAL CORRIDOR
During the Second World War (1939-1945) Sunderland and Catalina Flying Boats from RAF Castle Archdale were given permission by the neutral Irish Free State government to fly along the River Erne between Belleek and Ballyshannon. This was known as the Donegal Corridor. Young airmen flew out to the mid-Atlantic to give protection to shipping convoys. A number of planes crashed in the locality. This plaque is in memory of the airmen and seamen from America, Australia, New Zealand, Canada, Britain and Ireland who lost their lives in the Battle of the Atlantic.

The Belleek Plaque

to the northern boundary of Rathlin O'Beirne Island, Carrigan Head, Saint John's Point and Pettigoe, and the southern boundary of Inishmurray and the south bank of Lough Melvin. Plaques on Ballyshannon Bridge and at Belleek record the agreement *(picture)*.

The first official flight took place on 21 February 1941, when a Supermarine Stranraer went out to escort the British steamer SS *Jessmore*, which had been torpedoed by a U-boat. On the basis of further negotiations, land-based aircraft were permitted to take advantage of the agreement.

Donegal Corridor

The new flight path, straight over the River Erne and into the Atlantic, became known as the 'Donegal Corridor'. Although there was no

formal agreement on Allied aircraft overflying Inishowen and other
parts of north Donegal, this was accepted by the Irish government,
as was the basing of a flying-boat refuelling tanker off Moville and a
tanker to refuel escort ships.

Some aircraft had to make emergency landings on Irish
airfields or, in the case of flying-boats, on lakes or coastal bays,
due to running low in fuel, or other causes. They were all refuelled
and took off again for base. Any aviation fuel taken from Irish
stocks was immediately replaced by the British authorities.

Atlantic Convoys

Lough Erne had been photographed by German reconnaissance
aircraft at the start of the war. When informing the Germans about
the Donegal Corridor, the Eire government made it clear that the
flight path was to be used by aircraft only for air-sea-rescue missions
for planes or vessels in distress, regardless of their country of origin.
However, the Germans were aware of the use of the corridor by the
Allies for operational purposes against their U-boats. In his radio
broadcast 'Germany Calling' William Joyce ('Lord Haw–Haw')
referred to the flying-boats as 'swans on Lough Erne'.

When Irish ships joined the Allied convoys on the north
Atlantic route, they were clearly marked with the letters 'Eire'
and flew the Irish flag. Notwithstanding, some were torpedoed
and sunk by the U-boats. In the course of a few years the Irish
ships saved some 700 British merchant seamen from drowning
in the Atlantic.

The *Bismarck*

On 26 May 1941, just a few short months after the establishment
of the Donegal Corridor, the German
battleship *Bismarck* was sunk in the
Atlantic with the loss of over 2,000 of its
crew; barely 200 survived. The battleship
(picture) was spotted by a Spitfire between
Norway and Iceland when making her run
from the German port of Hamburg into

the North Sea and the Atlantic but soon escaped from observation. On her run down the Atlantic, she sank the pride of the Royal Navy, the battlecruiser HMS *Hood,* and badly damaged the new battleship HMS *Prince of Wales.*

Two Catalinas from RAF Castle Archdale were deployed on a cross-over patrol on the battleship's likely routes to the French coast. It was known that the *Bismarck* was low on fuel and would have to head for port. Both aircraft used the Donegal Corridor and are recorded in the logbooks of the Irish coast-watching service. One of the Catalinas spotted the *Bismarck* through a break in the cloud. Braving heavy gunfire, the plane kept the battleship under observation until it was relieved by the other Catalina.

The might of the Royal Navy then assembled for an attack on the *Bismarck.* A torpedo from a Swordfish biplane flying from the aircraft carrier HMS *Ark Royal* struck the rudder of the *Bismarck.* This resulted in the battleship being able to move only in large circles and so she became an easy target for the attacking ships.

Treaty Ports

Following the establishment of the Irish Free State, three deepwater 'Treaty Ports' at Castletown Berehaven (in Bantry Bay), Queenstown (modern Cobh) and Lough Swilly were retained by the United Kingdom under the 1921 Anglo-Irish Treaty. The main reason for doing so was the fear that the German U-boat campaign around Irish coasts in 1914–18 might re-occur. Notwithstanding, as part of the resolution of the Anglo-Irish trade war in the 1930s, the three ports were returned to Ireland in 1938.

When Germany overran France, the west coast of Scotland and the south and east of Ireland came within easy striking distance of the *Luftwaffe* air bases and U-boat pens in France. The dangers of this situation were realised when the *Luftwaffe* attacked Glasgow and Clydeside on 13/14 March 1941. In addition German planes (supposedly by mistake) dropped bombs on Wexford, Carlow and Dublin in 1941.

The terrible blitz on Belfast in April and May 1941, aimed primarily at the destruction of the armaments factories, demonstrated how German planes were able to reach Belfast by flying up the Irish Sea from bases in France and across the north of England from bases in the Low Countries. When an appeal was made from Belfast to de Valera for assistance with fire fighting, he immediately ordered all available fire appliances from Dublin, Dundalk and Drogheda to go to the aid of the Belfast Fire Service.

Declaration of neutrality

No neutral European country declared war on Germany in wartime without first being attacked. At the outbreak of war Eire adopted a policy of 'benevolent neutrality'. Its territorial boundary was indicated by EIRE being painted in large white letters around the coast with large numbers indicating location.

While de Valera bore the brunt of the criticism placed on Eire by Britain for its stance, he had the full support not only of his

own party but also of most elected members of the opposition parties. There was also strong pressure on de Valera from the USA to cease the policy of neutrality, even though America remained neutral until Germany declared war on the country at the end of 1941.

While foreign policy decisions can take a long time to sort out, the Eire government responded in a matter of weeks to the British request in 1941 for flying-boats to fly over Donegal. This was an indication of how willing de Valera and the Irish people were to help their neighbours across the channel 'in their hour of greatest need'. He also regarded the flying boat men as "mariners in distress" when they crashed in Eire and were not interned, but allowed to return to their bases.

Castle Archdale

Castle Archdale was the ancestral home of the Archdale family, one of the Plantation 'undertakers' of the 17th century who came from Stafford, England. The castle was built in 1773, with a fine view of Lough Erne and the Magho Mountain. Behind the house was a large courtyard, where the farming activities were centred. The castle and land were requisitioned in 1941 and the family moved to other accommodation, never to return. The castle was knocked down in the 1970s but the courtyard has been restored and now forms part of a popular country park with a visitors centre and museum.

The principal role of the base was to provide cover for the convoys crossing the Atlantic. Construction work started in August 1941. New roads were built, trees felled and buildings erected. Nissen huts sprang up everywhere to accommodate personnel. A slipway, sheds and hangars were erected. A battery of 12 light anti- aircraft guns was based at Drumbo, carefully camouflaged to conceal the guns. The work was completed by January 1942.

The castle was used as the station HQ and quarters for the officers. A control tower was built on the roof. The top left hand window was widened to help with traffic control. A large green wall map with grid squares of the Atlantic dominated the control room.

Security on the Upper and Lower Loughs was the responsibility of a detachment of Royal Engineers, known as the 'Lough Erne Navy'. Three patrol boats kept the waters clear for the flying-boats and guarded against sabotage.

The base, along with the neighbouring bases at Killadeas and St Angelo, were under the command of a Group Captain from No. 15 Group RAF Coastal Command. Castle Archdale was home at varying times to the RAF's Nos. 119, 201, 202, 209, 228 and 240 Squadrons and the RCAF's Nos. 422 and 423 Squadrons. The longest serving squadrons were Nos. 201 and 423.

Keeping the flying-boats in the air required an enormous support effort by the ground crews. The planes had to be serviced on their return by the engine, air frame, radio, instrument and radar technicians and armourers checked the depth charges and guns.

The marine craft section looked after the pinnaces, tenders, launches and dinghies. In the event of crashes, the planes had to be salvaged with the help of Henry McGarry and his team of civilian boat builders, who were under contract for this purpose, and for the maintenance of the moorings.

The Women's Auxiliary Air Force (WAAF) provided secretarial, catering and medical services. Many women were employed as drivers and vehicle mechanics and in signals and radio.

Imperial War Museum CH 18021

An airwoman chalks up details of Coastal command's last patrol on the operations board at Castle Archdale.

Lough Erne was subject to seasonal rises and fall, as levels were controlled at the sluice at Belleek. The lough had not been fully surveyed prior to being commissioned, so that rocks and small islands located immediately below the surface were covered and uncovered according to the level of the lake. These proved particularly hazardous for aircraft taking off and landing in poor visibility.

Between 1941 and 1945 the flying-boats from Castle Archdale and Killadeas were involved in destroying at least six U-boats and damaging five others. No. 201 Squadron sank two U-boats, No. 422 Squadron also sank one and No. 423 Squadron sank three. Many U-boats were damaged, forcing them to return to their bases for repair. In some instances Royal Navy warships were also involved. Significantly, statistics relating to U-boat losses must be treated with caution because the precise circumstances of a number of sinkings will never be known. Sadly, four Fermanagh-based Sunderlands were shot down, three by U-boats and, mistakenly in one case, by 'friendly fire' from a convoy, while another blew up after ditching near a convoy.

360 young airmen who served in the bases died in action or in crashes, while many were lost at sea and have no known graves.

The first crash of a plane from Lough Erne was that of a Catalina which crashed on Anaugh Hill, Glenade, County Leitrim on 21 March 1941; all the crew were killed. The first plane to be re-fuelled at the coast was a Saunders-Roe Lerwick flying-boat which landed in Bundoran Bay on 10 April 1941. It was towed to the shore by local fishermen and skippered by Denis Briggs who was later involved in sighting the *Bismarck*. Fuel was brought by lorry from Castle Archdale and the plane took off for base. On 5 December 1941 a Catalina landed on Lough Gill, County Sligo, and again was re-fuelled to enable it to return to base.

A Pan Am Clipper aircraft landed at Castle Archdale on 17 June 1942 while taking Queen Wilhelmina of the Netherlands to New York.

Killadeas

Flying boats over Killadeas

Killadeas performed an important training role. It was home to No. 131 Operational Training Unit, No. 302 Ferry Training Unit and No. 272 Maintenance Unit.

Killadeas overlooks Goblusk Bay, a wide expanse of water, which had been used by the Fermanagh gentry to race their yachts before the outbreak of war *(picture)*. The bay was ideal for training pilots to fly flying-boats. Pilots learned to deal with situations such as stalling in the air, single-engine flying and engine failure after take off.

Situated opposite to Killadeas in the bay was a large slipway *(picture)* on which the flying-boats were hauled out for servicing and repair.

In May 1944 a satellite unit was established on Boa Island (famous for its two-faced Early Christian stone Janus figure) for operational training exercises. A bombing range quadrant tower was erected at Dreenan on the western side of the island close to the shore.

Today the site of the old Training Unit is the home of the Lough Erne Yacht Club.

St Angelo

Originally known as Rosahilly, St Angelo (named after the bishop's residence) was the only airfield in Fermanagh with a hardcore runway. The site was chosen to be developed as No. 18 Satellite Landing ground for the storage of aircraft under the auspices on No. 23 Maintenance Unit at RAF Aldergrove, but was little used as such.

A perceived need for the flying-boat bases at Castle Archdale and Killadeas to be protected by fighters resulted in St Angelo being transferred to Fighter Command in September 1941. However, no aircraft arrived until December, when a few Spitfires of No. 133 Squadron arrived on a brief detachment from their base at Eglinton. From time to time, for short periods, small numbers of Spitfires were detached from Ballyhalbert, County Down.

It was not until February 1944 that St Angelo's usefulness for fighter defence purposes was vindicated. To counter particularly worrying *Luftwaffe* attacks on convoys by long range Dornier and Junkers 290 aircraft to the west of Ireland, 10 Beaufighters from No. 235 Squadron in Cornwall were based at St Angelo for most of that month; an enemy aircraft was shot down.

Meanwhile, from 1942 onwards, fortuitously, the airfield proved to be a diversionary haven to increasing numbers of aircraft on delivery to the UK from the USA, low on fuel, lost or otherwise in trouble. Various types transited, including Hudsons, Venturas, Liberators, Mitchells, C-47s and Fortresses.

The beacon on the tower of the nearby St Michael's Parish Church became a familiar landmark for pilots after their arduous flight across the Atlantic. After refuelling and time for the crews to rest, the aircraft usually flew on to bases in Great Britain, via the transatlantic ferry termini at Prestwick or Nutts Corner. Behind the church was a PoW camp.

The administrative HQ for No. 131 Operational Training Unit, Coastal Command, was located at St Angelo from 1942 until mid-1943; in August 1943 the airfield was transferred to RAF Coastal Command. Between October 1943 and April 1944 St Angelo housed the HQ of No. 422 Squadron, whose flying-boats were based at Castle Archdale.

In May 1944 No. 12 (Operational) Flying Instructors School was established at both Killadeas and St Angelo to train ex-operational pilots in instructor duties for service in Coastal Command training units; it remained there until June 1945. Between August 1945 and February 1947, No. 272 Maintenance Unit operated as a depot for the storage and salvage of Anson aircraft at St Angelo, as well as Catalina and Sunderland flying-boats at Killadeas.

Prince Bernhard of the Netherlands touched down at St Angelo on his way to the USA. When his plane could not take off because of bad weather, he spent the night at Necarne, where he was the guest of Captain R O Hermon.

St Angelo is now an airport owned by Fermanagh District Council. It is managed by a private company which offers facilities for visiting pilots and their aircraft, as well as training schools for microlight planes, light aircraft and helicopters.

4 OPERATIONS

Operating from Lough Erne, Consolidated Catalina and Short Sunderland flying-boats made an important contribution to the Battle of the Atlantic. The role of the flying-boats was to protect Allied convoys crossing the Atlantic. The surface escort group consisted usually of six to ten small warships, including frigates, sloops, corvettes and even trawlers.

Catalinas

The Catalinas were American and Canadian built. They were leased to the RAF as part of the lend-lease scheme by the American government. Some US personnel trained the RAF pilots and on occasions flew on operations with them.

The Catalina *(picture)* was a twin-engine, high-winged patrol flying-boat with retractable wing-tip floats. The power plant comprised a pair of Pratt and Whitney engines. There was also an amphibious version.

The Catalina was one of the first US aircraft to carry radar. At first this was a metric-wave radar with arrays of dipole antennae on the wings, but later changed to a centimetric radar in a fairing on top of the cockpit. A Leigh light was installed under the wing.

The plane had a range of up to 2,500 miles (4,000 km) and flew at 7,000 feet at speeds of up to 180 mph (290 km/h). It could stay airborne for as long as 28 hours.

Armament was five 0.50 calibre machine guns and eight depth charges.

The Catalina had a crew of nine to ten including three pilots, two of whom were at the controls while the third was resting. They sat side-by-side in a wide cockpit with large windows all round. The left and right gunner stations comprised blister windows on the waist of the hull behind the wing.

Twenty six Catalinas operating out of Lough Erne were lost at sea or in crashes.

Short Sunderlands

A large number of Sunderlands were built in Short and Harland of Belfast *(picture)*. The plane had four Bristol engines. The nose turret was later upgraded with a second .303 inch (7.7 mm) gun. New propellers together with pneumatic rubber wing de-icing boots were also fitted.

Although the .303 guns lacked range and hitting power, the Sunderland had a fair number of them. It was a well-built machine which was hard to destroy. The Germans nicknamed it the 'Flying Porcupine' due to its defensive firepower.

New weapons made the flying-boats more deadly in combat. Torpex-filled depth charges, which would sink to a pre-determined depth and then explode, were adopted.

A Leigh light was fitted to Sunderlands. New radar systems enabled the flying-boats to attack U-boats on the surface. Single 0.50 inch (12.7 mm) flexibly mounted M2 Browning machine guns also became common.

The crew was made up of the pilot, second pilot, navigator, three wireless operators, two flight engineers and a rigger. Wireless operators and flight engineers were also trained as air gunners.

A total of 192 airmen died in Sunderland crashes. Twenty seven Sunderlands were lost at sea or crashed, several in Lough Erne while on training exercises.

Imperial War Museum CH 18020

Patrols

For a typical mission in the early stages of the Battle of the Atlantic, the duty crew was woken between 2 and 3 am. After a breakfast of steak, bacon and eggs, the pilot, navigator and first wireless officer made their way to the operations room for briefing, while the remainder of the crew proceeded by pinnace to the plane to prepare for take-off. When ready, the flying boat was guided to the flight path by a pinnace displaying a rear light.

Arriving at the convoy at first light, the aircraft identified itself to the senior naval officer on duty, using either an Aldis lamp or light signal. The pilot was briefed about his task, including reports of any enemy activity. After a sweep of the convoy to count the vessels and any stragglers, the crew settled down to scan the sea for U-boats on the surface which were charging their batteries in preparation for an attack.

Flying at under 1,000 feet if visibility allowed, the crew took it in turn to use field glasses to identify U-boats, a monotonous task. Radio silence was maintained. If a U-boat was spotted, it was attacked with depth charges and gunfire.

In 1942, with the advent of the Leigh light, Coastal Command aircraft equipped with the light were enabled to attack U-boats on the surface at night, so that at no time could the enemy feel free from aerial attack.

The planes patrolled until darkness fell, at which point they took their leave of the convoy, wishing the senior naval officer good luck on his passage. Arriving back at Castle Archdale, the crew reported its safe return, having spent up to 18 hours on patrol.

When not engaged in convoy duties, the crews were required to maintain their skills in dropping bombs, using targets in Lough Neagh and the Gull Rock in Lough Erne.

Navigation aids

Aircraft flying to and from air bases in Fermanagh (and elsewhere in Northern Ireland) were able to make use of a variety of radio navigation aids. At Castle Archdale, Killadeas and St Angelo, homing procedures were based on high frequency direction finding facilities. At Castle Archdale there was also a radar responder blind approach beacon system (BABS). This was the basis of a let down and alighting procedure which was devised by a flying boat pilot and was unique to that base. Lights moored on Lough Erne defined the boundaries of the flying-boat alighting areas.

To facilitate aircraft on delivery from the USA to the transatlantic ferry terminal at Nutts Corner in County Antrim, there was a non-directional beacon at Derrynacross, near Garrison, operated by the RAF (coded UU7) and a four-course radio range at Magheramenagh operated by the USAAF (coded EC). US-trained pilots being heavily radio range oriented, Magheramenagh was complemented by a similar range close to Nutts Corner.

The two Fermanagh beacons also served as an approach facility, albeit to be used with care, by flying-boats operating over the Atlantic from Lough Erne and aircraft based at St Angelo or diverted to that airfield in transit from the USA.

Occasionally, use was made of radio navigation beacons in Eire, on Tory Island and Malin Head in County Donegal.

A ground controlled intercept radar station was erected at Drumlught, near Lisnaskea. There was another type of radar facility outside Newtownbutler.

Crashes

63 aircraft were lost as a result of flying operations from the three bases. When planes crash-landed in Eire, those killed were recovered by the Irish Army and brought to the border at Belleek. The bodies were handed over with full military honours to their comrades of the RAF.

Many crash sites all over Ireland have been marked with memorials in honour of those who died. These were erected by local people in the areas where the crashes happened out of respect for the families of those killed.

Passionist Monastery

One particular crash which occurred in Fermanagh is of especial poignancy. The scene of the crash was the Passionist Monastery at the Graan, on the outskirts of Enniskillen.

On the evening of 9 December 1943, as the Religious were preparing to have their evening meal in the company of their bishop, the sound of an aeroplane was heard circling overhead. The plane was a Boeing B-17 Flying Fortress, which had set out from Goose Bay, Newfoundland, 13 hours previously, destination Prestwick. (This four-engine heavy bomber was of a type used by the USAAF in the daylight strategic bombing campaign against German industrial and military targets.)

Named 'Gally Uncle', the aeroplane was heading for the monastery when it swerved and shot upwards. When coming down, its right wing struck a tree in the Folly Field, causing the plane to somersault, slide along the ground and burst into flames.

The Religious rushed to the scene and quickly put out the fire with their fire extinguishers. The rear gunner escaped with minor facial injuries. Three airmen were pulled from the plane alive, wrapped in the monastery's blankets and taken to hospital. Sadly seven airmen were killed.

Subsequent accident reports revealed that the aircraft, very low on fuel, had been diverted to St Angelo. The pilot, having only identified the airfield when overhead, was in the circuit attempting to land when the aircraft lost height rapidly due to failing engines and crashed. There is a memorial plaque on the grotto *(picture)* in the monastery grounds.

Social life

The greatest dampener on the spirits of the airmen was the weather – the incessant rain, low cloud base and absence of sun. The blackout added to the misery, with no street lights and a ban on car headlights. Rationing was another constraint; shops were not allowed to sell certain foods or clothing except on production of coupons. Petrol was also rationed. Some of the pain was offset by a vibrant cross-border smuggling trade.

In spite of the adverse influences on morale, personnel found time to relax when off duty. Fermanagh families welcomed the forces into their homes, offering hospitality. But for the most part the service men and women relied on sporting activities, in-camp entertainment and visits to local towns for entertainment.

The Stormont government organized 45 local 'hospitality committees' from September 1942 for the US troops, the Enniskillen committee being particularly energetic.

Groups got together to organise games, which included football, basketball, baseball, table tennis and (privately with local families) tennis, horse riding and duck shooting.

The NAAFI van drove around the camps, selling cigarettes, tea and cakes and the Entertainments National Service Association (ENSA) arranged live shows with leading showmen, including Joe Loss and his band. Messes ran dances, which were popular. Many romances blossomed, some leading to weddings. Married couples were allowed to live in lodgings. The Salvation Army (the 'Sally Ann') provided non-alcoholic drinks and a welfare service. In-house cinemas showed films. Games included housey-housey (bingo), cards, darts, etc.

On Saturdays a patrol boat ferried service personnel from Castle Archdale, Killadeas and St Angelo to Enniskillen. A liberty truck also operated from the bases. Films were shown in the Regal and Townhall cinemas. Hotels and cafes did a roaring trade.

Just four miles from Castle Archdale, Irvinestown *(picture 1944)* was a major attraction for the men and women in uniform. The town boasted 11 public houses, three hotels and a number of eating establishments. Dances were held in the Town Hall, Orange Hall and St Molaise Hall. A musical troop called the 'V Diggers' provided concerts. St Molaise Drama Group staged plays. A reading room offered books supplied by townspeople.

End of hostilities

VE Day in Europe, 8 May 1945, was marked by bonfires, church services, parties and dances organised by the civilian population.

Sunderland patrols continued into the Atlantic for another month after VE Day in case any U-boat commanders continued to attack Allied shipping.

The final operational patrol of the war by RAF Coastal Command was on 3/4 June 1945 and was carried out from Castle Archdale by No. 201 Squadron *(picture)*. The patrol, appropriately crewed by a composite group of Australians, New Zealanders, Canadians and Britons, escorted an inbound convoy of 51 ships.

By the end of June 1945 Castle Archdale had gone over to peacetime operations. On 18 August 1945 Castle Archdale was closed down and, by the end of the month, all operational squadrons had left the base. Some of the flying-boats which were no longer required were sold as scrap, while others are said to have been scuttled in the deep parts of the Lough at Killadeas.

Occasional use was made of Castle Archdale in post-war years by RAF Sunderlands and their crews while taking part in training courses run by the Joint Anti-Submarine School at HMS *Sea Eagle* in Londonderry.

Graves

A total of 320 men died in 41 missions involving Lough Erne flying-boats. Graves and memorials of personnel killed during the war are to be found in all parts of the county. Their names are recorded in a Roll of Honour in Fermanagh.

The greatest number of graves is to be found in the Church of Ireland Parish Church in Irvinestown *(opposite)*. The graveyard contains the remains of 74 airmen from the Commonwealth,

Imperial War Museum CH 15350

mainly Canada, Australia and New Zealand; 26 are buried in front of the church, where there is also a large Cross of Sacrifice, while 48 are buried behind the church. All are kept in immaculate condition. Ten Roman Catholic airmen are buried in the graveyard of the nearby Sacred Heart Church. Most of the bodies of the RAF men were returned to their families in Britain.

The funeral of the crew from the 201 Squadron Sunderland, August 1943

5   US ARMY

Military Bases

As the war progressed, and with no sign of an early end, land was requisitioned throughout Northern Ireland at the large estates. The owners were compensated for the loss of their land and use of their houses. The Ministry of Information claimed that 300,000 US troops 'passed through' Northern Ireland between 1942 and 1944.

To accommodate the troops, hundreds of semi-cylindrical, corrugated steel Nissen huts (sleeping up to 30 but usually cold and damp) and facilities buildings were erected. Shooting ranges and obstacle courses were built for training purposes.

The estates requisitioned in Fermanagh to accommodate American forces included

Ashbrook	Colebrooke	Ely Lodge
Breandrum	Crom Castle	Irvinestown
Belle Isle	Derrygonnelly	Killadeas
Castle Coole	Drumcose Estate	Lisgoole Abbey

Imperial War Museum H 15207

Exercises at Crom Castle, November 1941.

Operation TORCH

The first American troops to come to Fermanagh arrived in 1942 under Operation MAGNET. Elements of the 34th (later known as 'Red Bull') Infantry (Mechanised) Division, part of V Corps, were based at St Angelo, Crom (near Newtownbutler), Castle Coole and in Enniskillen. More were in Necarne Castle (Irvinestown) and on the Ely Lodge estate. They trained in the rugged mountain area of the Bar of Wealt (now Lough Navar Forest Park) and other parts of Fermanagh. Between September and October 1942 the fighting men departed for Operation TORCH, the invasion of French North-West Africa.

An administrative unit remained to prepare for the arrival of the second wave of US troops in 1943.

Operation OVERLORD

XV Corps began to arrive in late 1943 to prepare for the Normandy landings. The Corps consisted of 2nd US Infantry Division (with their proud claim to be 'second to none'), 5th Infantry Division (the 'Red Diamonds'), 8th Infantry Division (the 'Pathfinders') and 82nd Airborne Division. By February 1944 there were 100,000 American soldiers in Northern Ireland.

The 8th Infantry Division was a mechanised infantry division which went by the nickname of the 'Golden Arrow' Division and, later, the 'Pathfinder' Division. Both titles were taken from the vertical gold arrow in the formation's shoulder patch.

The 8th Division's three infantry regiments – 13th, 121st and 28th – were among the US Army's best-known formations. The disposition of the regiments was as follows: HQ at Omagh; 13th Infantry Regiment at Ely Lodge; 28th Infantry Regiment at Drumcose (near Ely Lodge);

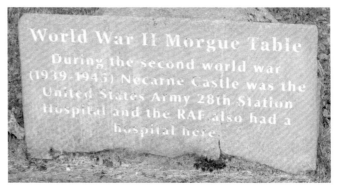

121st Infantry Regiment at Fintona (later at Ballynorthland, Dungannon) and the remainder at Ashbrook (Colebrooke).

General Dwight D Eisenhower reviewed the 28th Infantry Regiment on the playing fields of Portora Royal School, Enniskillen on 18 May 1944. He was accompanied by General William C McMahon, commander 8th Division. Lunch was taken in the 8th Infantry Division Club in the Royal Hotel, Enniskillen.

The division departed for France as part of Operation OVERLORD, landing on Omaha Beach, Normandy on 4 July and entering combat on 7 July 1944.

Necarne Hospital

Necarne Castle was used by the Americans and the RAF as a military hospital. The hospital originally had 200 beds but was soon enlarged to 500 beds.

The 28th Station Hospital moved into the castle grounds in the autumn of 1943 and left again in June 1944 for the invasion of France. A sole morgue table is the only relic from this period and a stone from the American base at Mageramena Castle bears testimony to this time.

There was no military presence in Fermanagh in 1939. The outbreak of war changed the situation dramatically. While the operations from the bases at Castle Archdale, Killadeas and St Angelo dominated the war effort, much else took place.

Enniskillen boasted two regiments whose names incorporated the old town name of 'Inniskilling'. Fermanagh was part of their recruiting territory and many men from the county were serving in the regiments when war broke out. Others were to join the Royal Navy, the Army and the Royal Air Force. Women also joined the women's services, making a valued contribution to the war effort.

By 1944 it was estimated that a quarter of the population was in uniform. There were, however, no barracks and recourse had to be made to Orange Halls and other local halls for accommodation.

Home Defence

Many men joined the Home Guard, while others joined the Ulster Special Constabulary, the B Specials. An Air Raids Precautions Unit was established to advise on responding to an air attack. Civil Defence detachments were formed and the National Fire Service established a presence. The Women's Voluntary Service formed units. Young men at the Technical School and Portora Royal School, Enniskillen, joined the Air Training Corps, which provided pre-entry training to the RAF and Fleet Air Arm. Detachments of the Red Cross and the St John Ambulance Brigade were raised.

The Royal Inniskilling Fusiliers

The 1st Inniskillings were in India at the outbreak of war in 1939. In 1942 the battalion was flown to Burma to help stem the Japanese advance and in 1943 took part in the operations in the Arakan peninsula.

The 2nd Battalion was part of the British Expeditionary Force and was among those evacuated from Dunkirk in 1940. After refitting, the battalion was sent to North Africa. Their journey took them to Syria, Persia, India and Madagascar, eventually arriving in the Mediterranean in time to take part in the invasion of Sicily, followed by that of Italy.

5th Royal Inniskilling Dragoon Guards

In 1938, as part of the preparation for war, the regiment was mechanised and, in the following year, became part of the newly-formed Royal Armoured Corps.

The regiment was part of the British Expeditionary Force which was forced to evacuate from Dunkirk in France in 1940. The Dragoon Guards remained in the UK until 1944, when they landed in Normandy a month after D Day, 6 June 1944, and took part in the advance by 7th Armoured Division (the famed 'Desert Rats') through France, Belgium and Germany. In July 1945 they participated in the Victory Parade in Berlin.

North Irish Horse

In 1939 the regiment was reformed as part of the Supplementary Reserve. Lord Erne raised a detachment in Fermanagh. In 1943 the regiment joined the First Army in North Africa, distinguishing itself in the campaign which ended in the capture of Tunis. The following year it took part in the Allied advance through Italy and saw action in the breaking of the Hitler Line in May 1944, followed by the advance on Florence and then the attack on the Gothic Line. It was also involved in the final attack in Italy, the advance to the Po in April 1945. A number of the officers and troopers were from Fermanagh.

British Army units

Throughout the war many British Army units came to Northern Ireland for battle preparation. Among those billeted in Fermanagh were: Royal Artillery; 2nd Royal Fusiliers; Leicesters; Cheshires; Glosters; 8th Sherwood Foresters; 2nd Northamptonshires; Ox and Bucks Light Infantry; The Bucks; Royal Berkshires; and Seaforth Highlanders. After the Americans left in June 1944, the 9th Buffs Infantry Training Battalion came to Ely Lodge and stayed there until the end of the war.

Field Marshals

Two distinguished Field Marshals in the Second World War had strong connections with Fermanagh.

Field Marshal Lord Alanbrooke, who had family connections with the Brooke family of Colebrooke, Brookeborough, was Chief of the Imperial General Staff for most of the war and Winston Churchill's principal military adviser.

Field Marshal Sir Claude Auchinleck had family connections with the Auchinlecks, an Ulster-Scots family from Fermanagh. Nicknamed 'The Auk', he spent much of his military career in India. A leading exponent of armoured warfare, he was Commander in Chief of the Middle East theatre from 1941 to 1942. He was Colonel of the Royal Inniskilling Fusiliers from 1941 to 1947.

The Evacuees

Fermanagh was home to many children who were evacuated from Belfast after the blitz in April and May 1941. Protestant children were billeted with Protestant householders and Roman Catholic children with Roman Catholic hosts. In most cases the boys and girls were treated as members of the family and attended local schools. As the threat of further bombing by the *Luftwaffe* diminished, the children were returned to their parents. Some of the children returned later in life to live in Fermanagh. Others were adopted by families and never went back to Belfast.

Acknowledgements

With thanks to Breege McCusker, Ian Henderson, Guy Warner and Ernie Cromie for permission to publish extracts from their books:

- *Castle Archdale and Fermanagh in World War II* by Breege McCusker
- *After the Battle. No 34: The GIs in Northern Ireland* by Ian Henderson
- *Military Aviation in Northern Ireland* by Guy Warner and Ernie Cromie.

Useful information about Fermanagh's airfields is contained in David J Smith's *Action Stations: 7. Military airfields of Scotland, the North-East and Northern Ireland*, Patrick Stephens, Cambridge, 1983.

Joe O'Loughlin is the author of *Catalinas and Sunderlands on Lough Erne in World War Two*, Choice Publishing and Book Services Ltd, Drogheda, 2013.

The rights of Joe O'Loughlin and John Hughes to be identified as the authors of this work have been asserted by them in accordance with the Copyright, Design and Patents Act 1988.

Every attempt has been made to contact picture credit holders. Credits are noted by the relevant picture. If there is no picture credit the picture belongs to the NIWM collection or is in the public domain. We welcome any new information about photographs featured in this publication.

Canadians from a far off land
Extended to us a helping hand
Catalinas set forth in the dead of night
Valiant men off to the fight.

For freedom and the defence of you and I
True heroes of land sea and sky
Sunderlands too – along the Donegal Corridor fly
Mighty thunder of the engines, through clouds high.

Called to arms to go and serve
With great courage and great nerve
What must have been a wonderful sight?
In the early mist of morning light.

Ooh what stories you could tell
As you flew into the jaws of hell
For some there will be no return
And those with regret we will mourn.

These men so generous – gave their all
In answer to this nation's call
Who are now fleeting spirits passing through
Blessed by deeds they did do.

Crew and comrades in eternal sleep
At rest in Lough Erne's waters deep
Who now await the trumpet's roar
And will reply to the flag once more.

This memorial in your name
Enshrined in our hearts you will remain
So soft rain keeps green the fern
Another day dawns over the Lough of Erne.

Helene Turner

*This poem is set beside two memorial stones at Lough Navar view point
in memory of the crews of two planes from Lough Erne*

Joe O'Loughlin is a local historian and author in Belleek, County Fermanagh, where he has lived all his life. Since retiring from his family business in 1997, he has developed his long-standing interest in local history, specialising in the Second World War. Joe is a member of the Clogher and Donegal Historical Societies.

John Hughes (1939 – 2013) grew up in Irvinestown and Enniskillen and then settled in Holywood Co. Down. He served in the Territorial Army, including the Royal Inniskilling Fusiliers, and the Ulster Defence Regiment. He commanded Queen's University Officers' Training Corps.

John was the Secretary of the Northern Ireland War Memorial. For nine years he put his heart and soul into every aspect of the organisation and management of the museum. John recognised that the new building in Talbot Street would be an ideal replacement for the ageing original War Memorial on Waring Street. He recruited a staff to create a gallery that would illustrate the wartime role of Northern Ireland and the tragic losses in the air raids. He was involved in the restoration of the graves of the unknown dead. He commissioned a series of publications telling the story of wartime Northern Ireland. He proofread every one meticulously and maintained close contact with the media, ensuring that the War Memorial was frequently in the news.

He will be greatly missed, however the Northern Ireland War Memorial will always be John's memorial.

John Potter
Patron of Northern Ireland War Memorial